J 523.113 Mil
The Milky Way.

34028081098924
CYF $25.90 ocn460710825
10/24/12

3 4028 08109 8924
HARRIS COUNTY PUBLIC LIBRARY

D1314215

Explore the Universe
THE MILKY WAY

WORLD
BOOK

a Scott Fetzer company
Chicago
www.worldbookonline.com

World Book, Inc.
233 N. Michigan Avenue
Chicago, IL 60601
U.S.A.

For information about other World Book publications, visit our Web site at **http://www.worldbookonline.com** or call **1-800-WORLDBK (967-5325)**.

For information about sales to schools and libraries, call **1-800-975-3250 (United States)**, or **1-800-837-5365 (Canada)**.

© 2010 World Book, Inc. All rights reserved. This volume may not be reproduced in whole or in part in any form without prior written permission from the publisher.

WORLD BOOK and the GLOBE DEVICE are registered trademarks or trademarks of World Book, Inc.

Library of Congress Cataloging-in-Publication data
The Milky Way.
    p. cm. -- (Explore the universe)
    Includes index.
    Summary: "An introduction to the Milky Way with information about its formation and characteristics. Includes diagrams, fun facts, glossary, resource list, and index"--Provided by publisher.
    ISBN 978-0-7166-9550-9
    1. Milky Way--Juvenile literature. I. World Book, Inc.
    QB857.7.M54 2010
    523.1'13--dc22
                        2009042566

ISBN 978-0-7166-9544-8 (set)
Printed in China by Leo Paper Products LTD.
   Heshan, Guangdong
1st printing February 2010

STAFF

Executive Committee:
President: Paul A. Gazzolo
Vice President and Chief Marketing Officer: Patricia Ginnis
Vice President and Chief Financial Officer: Donald D. Keller
Vice President and Editor in Chief: Paul A. Kobasa
Vice President, Licensing & Business Development: Richard Flower
Managing Director, International: Benjamin Hinton
Director, Human Resources: Bev Ecker
Chief Technology Officer: Tim Hardy

Editorial:
Associate Director, Supplementary Publications: Scott Thomas
Managing Editor, Supplementary Publications: Barbara A. Mayes
Senior Editor, Supplementary Publications: Kristina A. Vaicikonis
Manager, Research, Supplementary Publications: Cheryl Graham
Manager, Contracts & Compliance (Rights & Permissions): Loranne K. Shields
Editors: Michael DuRoss, Brian Johnson
Writer: Darlene Stille
Indexer: David Pofelski

Graphics and Design:
Manager: Tom Evans
Coordinator, Design Development and Production: Brenda B. Tropinski
Senior Designer: Don Di Sante
Photographs Editor: Kathy Creech

Pre-Press and Manufacturing:
Director: Carma Fazio
Manufacturing Manager: Steven K. Hueppchen
Production/Technology Manager: Anne Fritzinger
Proofreader: Emilie Schrage

Cover Illustration:
The Milky Way rises like a great river of light over Devils Tower National Monument in Wyoming. The disk of the Milky Way actually forms a circle that completely surrounds Earth. Clouds of dust and gas hide some of the stars in the disk.

© Wally Pacholka, AstroPics

CONTENTS

If a word is printed in **bold letters that look like this,** that word's meaning is given in the glossary on pages 60-61.

INTRODUCTION

On dark nights, a great river of stars rises from the horizon. There are so many stars in this river that they appear as a single band of white that straddles the sky. We call this river the Milky Way.

For as long as human beings have lived, they have watched the night sky and wondered about the Milky Way. Today, we know that the Milky Way is actually a vast galaxy containing hundreds of billions of stars. These stars extend in great spiral arms from the galaxy's core. The solar system lies on one of these arms, about halfway between the galaxy's center and its edge.

Using modern telescopes, astronomers have learned that the Milky Way is full of wonders beyond number. Great clouds of dust and gas give birth to stars. Other stars die in mighty explosions. Through the ages, the Milky Way slowly circles like a magnificent wheel, filling the heavens with light.

Stars numbering in the billions shine through clouds of dust and gas at the center of the Milky Way.

WHAT IS THE MILKY WAY?

A SPECIAL GALAXY

The Milky Way is just one of billions of **galaxies** in the universe. But the Milky Way is special to us because it is our home galaxy. The **solar system**—the sun and all its planets—are in the Milky Way. Because the Milky Way is our home, it is sometimes just called the galaxy.

The solar system is not in the center of the galaxy. The sun and its **planets** are about halfway between the center and the edge of the Milky Way.

A PINWHEEL IN SPACE

The Milky Way is a **spiral galaxy,** shaped like a pinwheel. Other galaxies have different shapes. Some are **elliptical** (ball-shaped) **galaxies.** Some are classified as **irregular galaxies.** They do not have any particular shape.

At night, the Milky Way appears as a glowing band arching across the sky.

The Milky Way is a galaxy, a huge grouping of stars, dust, gas, and other matter held together in space by their mutual gravitational pull.

Long, curving arms of stars, dust, and gas spiral out from the central disk of the Milky Way.

HOW DID THE MILKY WAY GET ITS NAME?

SKY WATCHING

In ancient times, the night was very dark. There were no street lights to make cities and villages bright. In the night sky, people could clearly see a broad white band of light stretching from horizon to horizon. Ancient people did not know it, but the band actually goes around Earth like a great white circle.

SPILLED MILK

The Milky Way is one of the most fascinating objects in the sky. The ancient Greeks thought the white band looked like spilled milk. They called it the Milky Circle. The ancient Romans called it the Milky Road. Over time, the name changed to the Milky Way.

DID YOU KNOW?

The ancient Greek philosopher Democritus, who lived from about 460 to 370 B.C., was the first known person to suggest that the Milky Way is made of stars.

In an ancient Chinese myth, the Milky Way is a river placed in the heavens by gods trying to separate a weaver who made their clothes and the herdsman who loved her.

The Milky Way appears as a circle of stars in an illustration from 1681.

Dr. M. Wilh. Meyer
Vom Himmel und von der Erde

An astronomer studies the Milky Way in an illustration used as the cover of a German book published in 1908.

IMAGES OF THE MILKY WAY

For tens of thousands of years, stargazers marveling at the magnificence of the Milky Way could not have suspected that there were equally brilliant views that were invisible to human eyes. Visible light, the light we can see, is only one form of energy given off by stars and other objects in the universe. The development of telescopes that can observe these other forms of light revolutionized astronomy.

Telescopes that collect infrared light can penetrate the vast clouds of dust and gas that block visible light from the center of the galaxy and reveal stars in the process of forming. In ultraviolet light, scientists can study the sun and the hydrogen between stars. Telescopes that "see" radio waves help scientists learn about powerful objects called pulsars and quasars. Gamma-ray images offer information about collapsed stars and the interactions between matter and antimatter. In addition to providing new details about stars and other known objects, all these telescopes have revealed many previously unknown objects, including black holes.

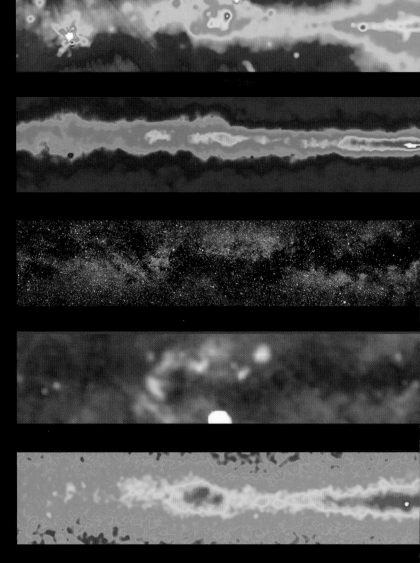

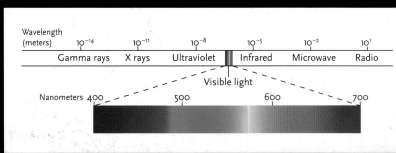

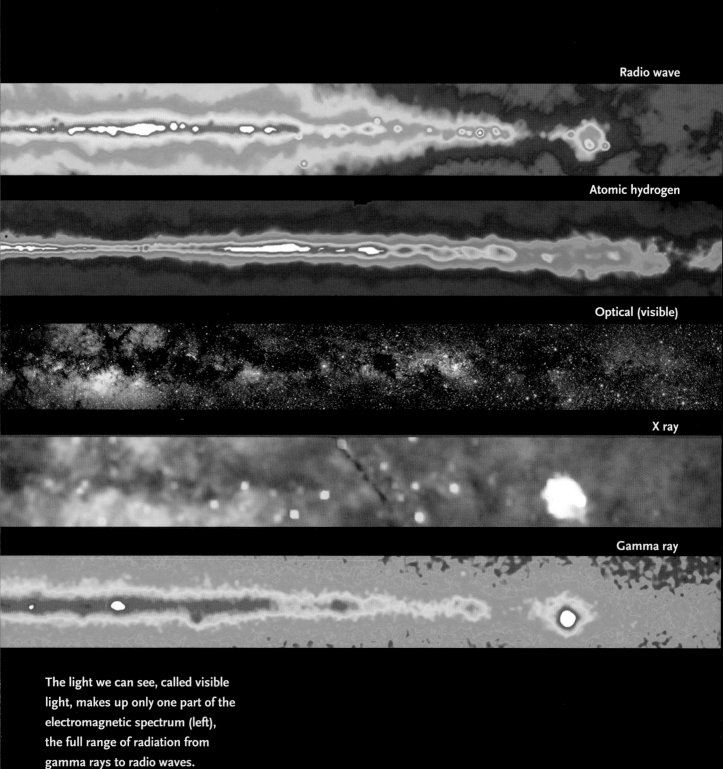

Radio wave

Atomic hydrogen

Optical (visible)

X ray

Gamma ray

The light we can see, called visible
light, makes up only one part of the
electromagnetic spectrum (left),
the full range of radiation from
gamma rays to radio waves.

STAR-FILLED SKY

People on Earth see the Milky Way as a fuzzy, glowing band of light in the sky. You are inside the Milky Way and looking through it. Because you are inside it, you have a very limited view of the **galaxy.** This view of our galaxy is like looking at the edge of a Frisbee.

LIGHT POLLUTION

In order to clearly see the white band of light, you need to be far from any city. People who live in or near big cities often see **stars** only faintly at night. That is because many cities in our modern world have grown so large and use so much artificial light at night. In many parts of the eastern United States and Canada, in parts of Europe, and in Japan, city dwellers often can see only a handful of the brightest stars, even on a clear, moonless night. Bright city lights blot out the faint light of most stars. This excess light is called **light pollution.**

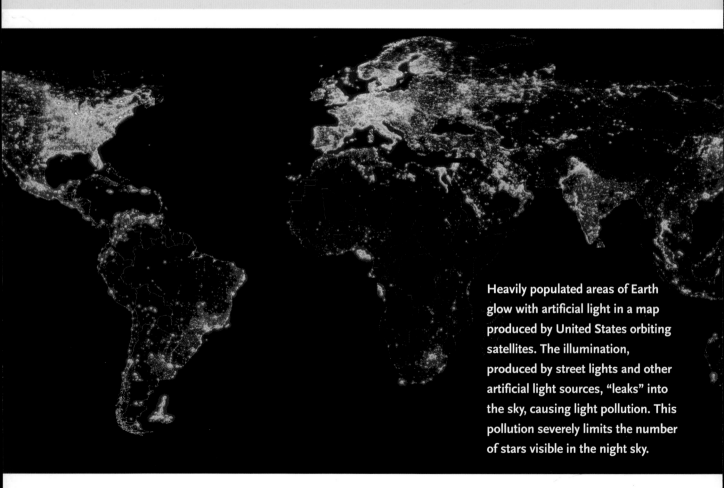

Heavily populated areas of Earth glow with artificial light in a map produced by United States orbiting satellites. The illumination, produced by street lights and other artificial light sources, "leaks" into the sky, causing light pollution. This pollution severely limits the number of stars visible in the night sky.

When you see the Milky Way in a dark night sky, you are seeing less than 1 percent of the galaxy's hundreds of billions of stars.

In 1908, the Los Angeles area was home to only 350,000 people, and light pollution was a limited problem for astronomers at the nearby Mount Wilson Observatory.

Today, more than 9 million people live in the Los Angeles area, and light pollution has become so severe that only the moon and the brightest stars are visible at night.

A BIG BLUR

Stars produce tremendous amounts of energy. They get this energy from **nuclear fusion** reactions occurring deep inside. In most stars, nuclear fusion joins the *nuclei* (cores) of **hydrogen** to produce a nucleus of **helium.**

From Earth, you see so many stars in the Milky Way from a variety of distances that they seem to be close together. The unaided eye cannot pick out most individual stars. Instead, the light from all the stars seems to blend together to create the blurry glow of a white band in the sky. Powerful telescopes, however, can observe most of the individual stars in the Milky Way.

Some of the most massive stars in the Milky Way are in the center of the galaxy, as seen in an infrared photograph taken by the Very Large Telescope in Chile.

DID YOU KNOW?

The sun and other stars are made of plasma, a gas-like form of matter composed of electrically charged particles.

The light from stars makes the Milky Way glow in the night sky.

The central bulge of the Milky Way blazes with light from billions of stars in a 360-degree image made from nearly 1,200 photographs taken over several weeks by observatories in Chile.

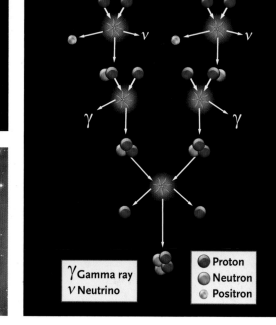

Stars get their energy from nuclear fusion. In a series of three reactions, four hydrogen nuclei fuse together to form one helium nucleus. At each step, particles and energy are released that help to drive the reaction.

γ Gamma ray
ν Neutrino

Proton
Neutron
Positron

PARTS OF THE MILKY WAY

For as long as people have looked toward the heavens, they have seen a strip of night sky more brilliant with stars than any other part. This strip of stars was named the MIlky Way long before its full nature was known. As telescopes became more powerful and versatile, a clearer picture of the true shape of the Milky Way began to emerge.

The three-dimensional structure of the galaxy is much clearer today than it was even a few decades ago. The "strip" of stars is just the disk of the galaxy seen edge on from Earth. We know the galaxy is somewhat flat, has a bulge in the middle, and has several arms (areas more dense with stars) that spiral out from the bulge. Scientists have also noticed small galaxies and even smaller clusters of stars drifting just beyond the Milky Way's edges. In more recent times, a thin ring of very old stars has been observed traveling around the outer reaches of the galaxy's disk.

Previously unobserved "streams" of stars from the dwarf galaxies move toward the Milky Way in a computer-generated image based on data from the Sloan Digital Sky Survey. ▼

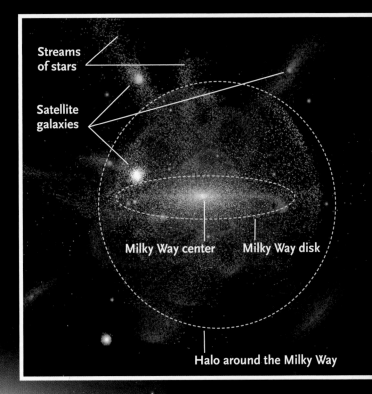

Streams of stars

Satellite galaxies

Milky Way center   Milky Way disk

Halo around the Milky Way

◀ Hundreds of billions of stars make up the Milky Way. Many of the most massive stars are in the innermost 1,000 light-years of the galaxy. The very center of the galaxy contains a powerful gravitational force that scientists believe is a black hole.

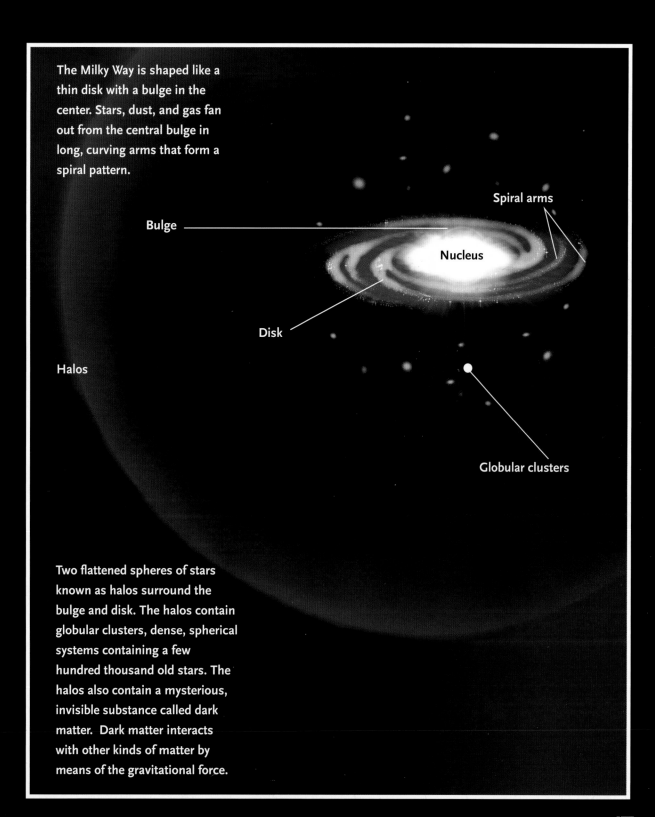

The Milky Way is shaped like a thin disk with a bulge in the center. Stars, dust, and gas fan out from the central bulge in long, curving arms that form a spiral pattern.

Spiral arms

Bulge

Nucleus

Disk

Halos

Globular clusters

Two flattened spheres of stars known as halos surround the bulge and disk. The halos contain globular clusters, dense, spherical systems containing a few hundred thousand old stars. The halos also contain a mysterious, invisible substance called dark matter. Dark matter interacts with other kinds of matter by means of the gravitational force.

HOW BIG IS THE MILKY WAY?

"YARDSTICK" OF LIGHT

Light travels through space at 186,282 miles (299,792 kilometers) per second. At this speed, light can cross a distance of about 5.88 trillion miles (9.46 trillion kilometers) in one year. Therefore, astronomers and physicists call the distance that light can travel in one year a **light-year.**

LIGHT-YEAR MEASUREMENTS

Astronomers estimate that the Milky Way is about 100,000 light-years across. They estimate that the central bulge is about 10,000 light-years thick, and the central bar is about 27,000 light-years long. But the thinner disk of the Milky Way is only about 1,000 light-years thick.

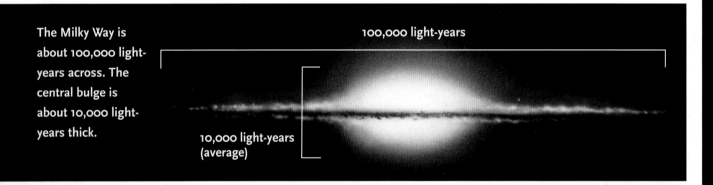

The Milky Way is about 100,000 light-years across. The central bulge is about 10,000 light-years thick.

100,000 light-years

10,000 light-years (average)

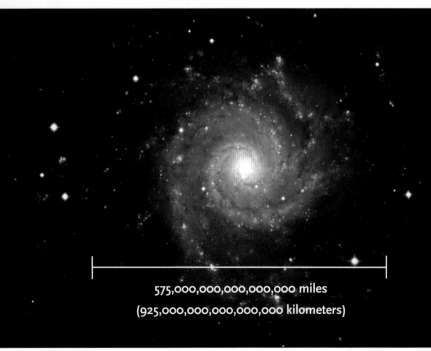

The galaxy M74 is much smaller than the Milky Way but closely resembles our galaxy in shape. Scientists study other spiral galaxies to understand more about our galaxy.

575,000,000,000,000,000 miles
(925,000,000,000,000,000 kilometers)

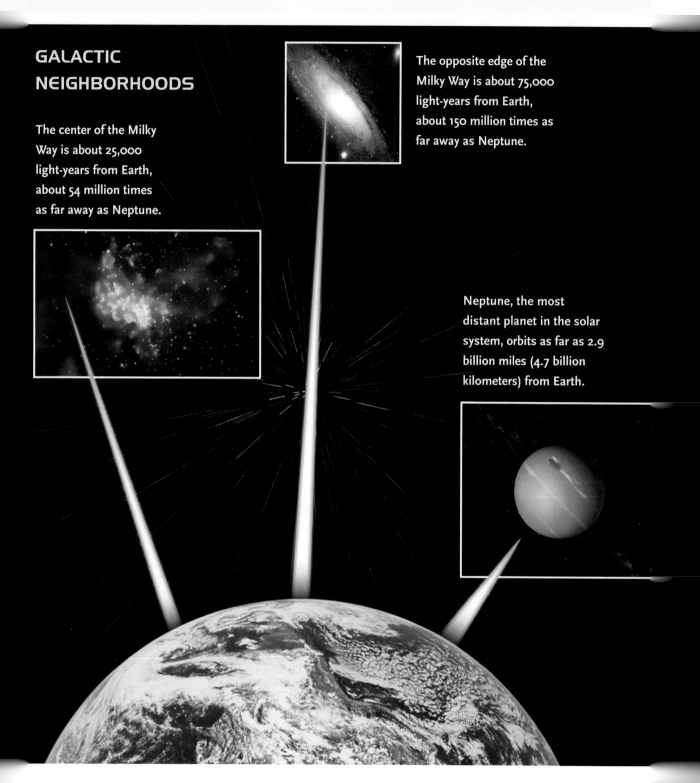

GALACTIC NEIGHBORHOODS

The center of the Milky Way is about 25,000 light-years from Earth, about 54 million times as far away as Neptune.

The opposite edge of the Milky Way is about 75,000 light-years from Earth, about 150 million times as far away as Neptune.

Neptune, the most distant planet in the solar system, orbits as far as 2.9 billion miles (4.7 billion kilometers) from Earth.

ORBITING ARMS

Like a spinning pinwheel, the spiral arms of the Milky Way rotate around the center of the **galaxy.** The central bar moves around its midpoint like a whirling propeller blade. The central bar and spiral arms move because the **stars** in them orbit the center of the Milky Way. The sun orbits the center of the galaxy at a speed of about 155 miles (250 kilometers) per second.

SPEEDING THROUGH SPACE

The entire Milky Way is also moving through space. In fact, the Milky Way and the nearby Andromeda Galaxy are approaching each other at about 75 miles (120 kilometers) per second. They will likely collide in several billion years. The 40 galaxies nearest to us also move as a group, sharing a speed of more than 930 miles (1,500 kilometers) per second in relation to more distant galaxies.

The spiral arms of the Milky Way rotate around the center of the galaxy.

DID YOU KNOW?

If Earth orbited the sun at the same speed that stars orbit the center of the Milky Way, our planet would travel around the sun in only 3 days instead of 365.

In addition to rotating around the center of the Milky Way, stars such as the sun *oscillate* (move up and down) through the plane of the galaxy.

The stars in the Milky Way move in a circular motion around the center of the galaxy. The whole galaxy also moves through space.

A galaxy with a comet-like tail 200,000 light-years long (arrow) speeds toward the center of a cluster of galaxies called Abell 3627 in an X-ray image taken by the Newton Space Observatory. Galaxies often collide and merge to form larger galaxies.

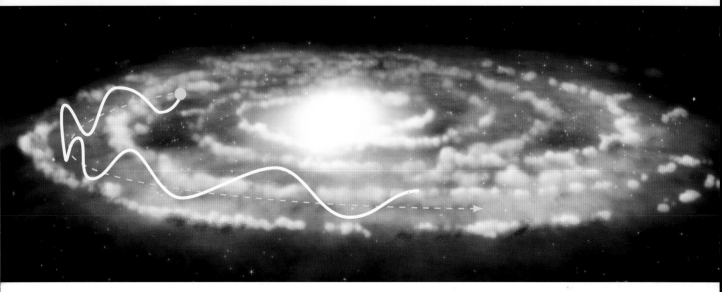

STAR CENTRAL

Stars in the Milky Way reach their greatest concentration at the center of the **galaxy.** In addition, the galactic center contains the most massive stars.

BLACK HOLE

There is a powerful force of **gravity** coming from something in the galaxy's center. Astronomers calculate that this force comes from an object with about 4 million times as much **mass** (amount of matter) as the sun. However, this object takes up only about as much space as the **solar system.** The only known object that could be so massive while being so small is a **black hole.**

A black hole is an object that contains a huge amount of matter packed into a small space. A black hole is a very dense object. The gravitational force of a black hole is so strong that not even light can escape. In addition, anything that comes too close to a black hole gets sucked into it, including stars.

ENERGY

Astronomers have also found **radio waves** and **X rays** coming from a source that they call Sagittarius A* in the very center of the galaxy. Such energy could come from gas being pulled into a supermassive black hole.

Vast clouds of gas and dust in the center of the Milky Way blaze with *infrared light* (heat energy) from massive young stars. At the very center of the galaxy is a supermassive black hole (inset) surrounded by a rotating ring of gas and dust.

The central bulge or bar of the Milky Way is tightly packed with millions of stars. There are also thick clouds of gas and dust and a massive black hole.

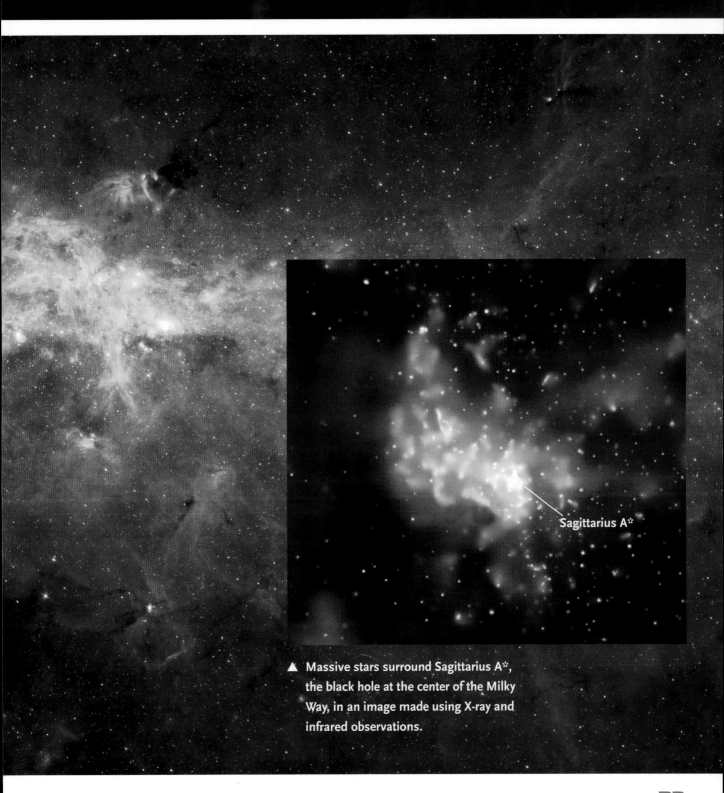

Sagittarius A*

▲ Massive stars surround Sagittarius A*, the black hole at the center of the Milky Way, in an image made using X-ray and infrared observations.

FINDING THE OLDEST STARS

Astronomers estimate the age of the **galaxy** by finding the age of its oldest **stars.** Most of the oldest stars are outside of the spiral arms that form the Milky Way's disk. Most of the youngest stars are in the spiral arms.

Astronomers estimate the age of stars by studying the **chemical elements** they contain. By analyzing the light coming from stars, astronomers can determine which chemical elements the stars are made of.

Globular clusters, such as NGC 6397 (below), contain some of the oldest stars in the Milky Way. Studies of the chemical elements in the stars of these relatively small, densely packed groups indicate that the stars formed shortly after the big bang, more than 13 billion years ago.

Astronomers believe that our galaxy is more than 13 billion years old. It is almost as old as the universe, which formed about 13.7 billion years ago.

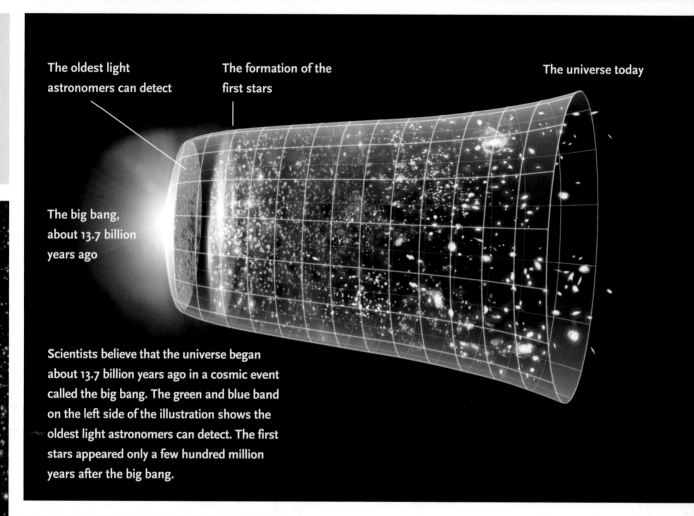

The oldest light astronomers can detect

The formation of the first stars

The universe today

The big bang, about 13.7 billion years ago

Scientists believe that the universe began about 13.7 billion years ago in a cosmic event called the big bang. The green and blue band on the left side of the illustration shows the oldest light astronomers can detect. The first stars appeared only a few hundred million years after the big bang.

ANSWERS IN THE ELEMENTS

The first stars formed from clouds of gas that contained only three light chemical elements— **hydrogen, helium,** and lithium. **Nuclear fusion** reactions inside the first stars created other, heavier elements.

The first stars in the Milky Way soon died in powerful explosions. The chemical elements in these stars then became part of the clouds of gas and dust left over from the explosions. Then, clumps of gas and dust pulled together because of **gravity** to form a new generation of stars containing such heavier elements as oxygen and iron. By studying and comparing amounts of different chemical elements, astronomers concluded that the oldest stars in the Milky Way—and, therefore, the Milky Way itself—are more than 13 billion years old.

WHERE IS EARTH IN THE MILKY WAY?

LIFE IN THE SUBURBS

The sun is located in the disk of the **galaxy,** along with Earth and everything else in the **solar system.** Astronomers have determined that the sun is about 25,000 **light-years** from the center of the galaxy, on a spiral arm called the Orion Spur. The sun is halfway between the center and the outer edge of the disk.

All **stars** in the Milky Way orbit the center of the galaxy. The sun completes a nearly circular orbit of the center about every 240 million years. Almost all the bright stars in the Milky Way orbit in the same direction. Thus, the entire galactic system rotates about its center.

Sun

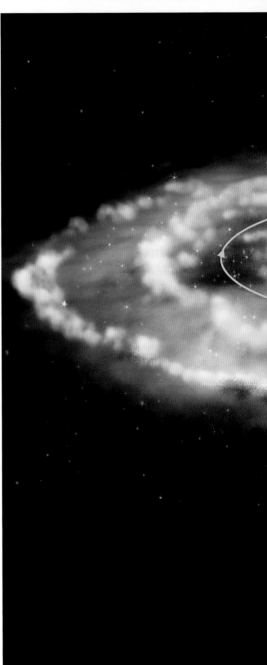

The sun orbits the center of the Milky Way along with other stars in our spiral arm. The sun completes an orbit every 240 million years.

Sun

The sun is about 25,000 light-years from the center of the Milky Way, halfway between the center and the edge of the galaxy's disk.

The sun is one of millions of stars in the Milky Way Galaxy.

Earth and the other planets of the solar system orbit the sun.

The Local Group belongs to an even larger collection of galaxies called the Local Supercluster. The supercluster is about 100 million light-years across.

The Milky Way is part of a group of about 40 galaxies called the Local Group, which is held together by mutual gravitational attraction.

Local Group

EXTRASOLAR PLANETS

In the 1990's, astronomers began finding **planets** in orbit around distant **stars.** They call planets outside of the solar system extrasolar planets or **exoplanets.** New and more-powerful telescopes and other tools allowed astronomers to find signs of these planets.

STRANGE STARS

Many of the exoplanets discovered so far orbit stars quite different from the sun. The first exoplanet found orbits a **pulsar.** A pulsar blasts out jets of energy. As the pulsar spins, the jets appear to flash on and off like a lighthouse beacon. Exoplanets also orbit **binary star systems,** which contain two stars. Exoplanets have also been found around **red dwarfs,** stars with far less *mass* (amount of matter) than the sun. However, as detection methods improve, astronomers expect to find many exoplanets in orbit around stars that resemble the sun.

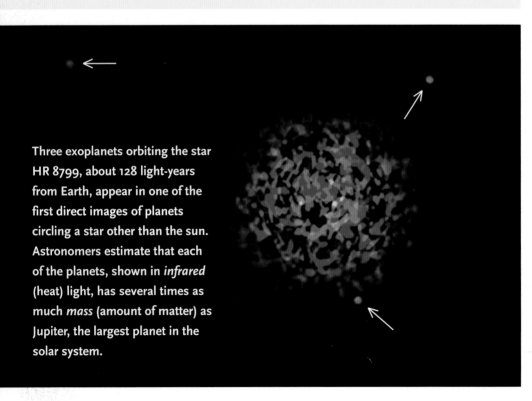

Three exoplanets orbiting the star HR 8799, about 128 light-years from Earth, appear in one of the first direct images of planets circling a star other than the sun. Astronomers estimate that each of the planets, shown in *infrared* (heat) light, has several times as much *mass* (amount of matter) as Jupiter, the largest planet in the solar system.

The sun is only one of hundreds of billions of stars in the Milky Way. Astronomers believe that many of these stars have planetary systems in orbit around them.

An exoplanet and its moons orbit the red dwarf star Gliese 876, about 15 light-years from the sun, as shown in an artist's illustration.

A RED DWARF

The nearest **star** to our solar system is Proxima Centauri, a **red dwarf** about 4.2 light-years away. It is much cooler and dimmer than the sun. The surface temperature of the sun is about 5,800 Kelvin (K) (10,000 °F). The surface temperature of Proxima Centauri is about 3,400 K (5,600 °F). Astronomers do not think that there is a **planetary system** around this star.

THREE-STAR SYSTEM

Proxima Centauri is part of a system of three stars called Alpha Centauri. The two other stars, Alpha Centauri A and Alpha Centauri B, are **binary stars.** They are close together in space and orbit each other. The brightest of these stars is Alpha Centauri A. It is about 4.4 light-years from Earth.

Proxima Centauri (center in the infrared image below) is the nearest star to the sun.

DID YOU KNOW?

If the Milky Way had the same diameter as a Frisbee, the thickness of the disk would be about that of a sheet of paper.

THE STARS OF ALPHA CENTAURI

Sun

Alpha Centauri A

Alpha Centauri B

Proxima Centauri is a red dwarf star, much smaller and dimmer than the sun.

Proxima Centauri

Proxima Centauri and the other two stars of Alpha Centauri (arrow) are so distant from Earth—about 4.4 light-years—that the system appears as a single star in the night sky.

GALILEO AND HIS TELESCOPE

In the 1600's, Italian astronomer and physicist Galileo became the first scientist to use a telescope in the practical service of astronomy. The telescope made distant objects look larger and clearer. Galileo saw details of the surface of the moon. He discovered moons orbiting Jupiter. He also discovered that the white band of light across the sky contains individual **stars.**

HERSCHEL AND HUBBLE

The next great advance in understanding the Milky Way came when British astronomer Sir William Herschel learned how to make ever-larger telescopes. Herschel looked deep into space and identified thousands of stars. Using this star catalog, he produced an early model of the Milky Way. He found that the sun is not fixed in space. He observed fuzzy cloud-like objects called **nebulae.** He speculated that these clouds might be "island universes" beyond the Milky Way. Finally, he discovered the existence of *infrared light* (heat energy), which became crucial to astronomy.

It was not until the 1920's that the American astronomer Edwin Hubble proved that the group of stars then called the Andromeda Nebula is outside the Milky Way. In fact, the Milky Way is only one among billions of galaxies. Hubble also found that other galaxies are in motion. The farther apart galaxies are, the faster they appear to be moving away from one another.

Italian astronomer and mathematician Galileo Galilei is known as the founder of modern experimental science.

Many astronomers contributed to our understanding of the Milky Way. However, until astronomers began using telescopes, little was known about the nature of our galaxy.

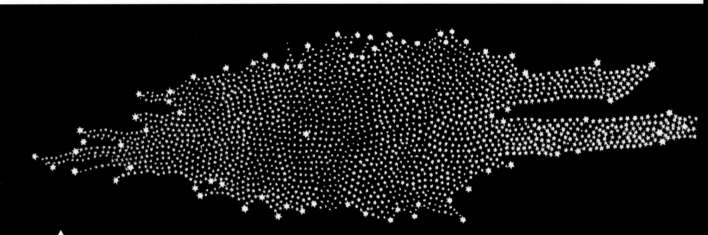

▲ A belief that the Milky Way was the entire universe led English astronomer Sir William Herschel to place the solar system in the middle of his 1785 map of the universe.

American astronomer Edwin Hubble proved that the Milky Way is only one among a large number of galaxies. ▶

WHAT HOLDS THE MILKY WAY TOGETHER?

Anyone who has seen an apple fall from a tree has observed **gravity** at work. The same force attracts all objects in the universe, including the stars of the Milky Way.

NEWTON'S THEORY

In the 1600's, English scientist Sir Isaac Newton developed the first modern theory of gravity. Newton realized that objects fall toward the center of Earth and **planets** orbit the sun due to one universal force called gravity. Newton described gravity as the attraction between two bodies. The strength of gravitational pull between two bodies depends upon their **mass** (amount of matter) and their distance.

EINSTEIN'S THEORY

Newton's theory works well in describing gravity at everyday scales. However, in the early 1900's, German-born American physicist Albert Einstein showed that Newton's theory breaks down at the largest scales. According to Einstein, gravity is actually a warp or bend in the structure of space itself.

Before Einstein, scientists thought that space was uniform, like a flat sheet of paper. Einstein found that massive objects such as stars bend space much as a bowling ball would create a dip in a soft mattress. A marble placed on the mattress would roll down toward the bowling ball. In a similar way, Earth is attracted toward the

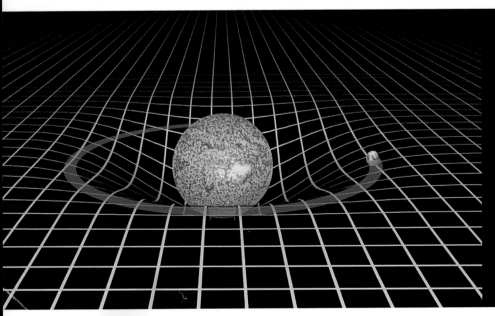

Albert Einstein found that gravity is actually a warp or bend in the structure of space itself. A planet orbits a star because it is caught in the bend made by the star's mass.

sun because of the bend the sun makes in space. Earth is traveling fast enough that it endlessly orbits the sun instead of plunging inward. However, Earth would have to travel much faster to climb out of the sun's gravitational well.

The hundreds of millions of stars in the Milky Way warp space on a scale that dwarfs the gravitational force of the sun. In fact, astronomers have found that the supermassive **black hole** Sagittarius A* sits at the very center of our galaxy. In a sense, the black hole rests at the lowest part of the bend made in space by our **galaxy.**

The collision of two enormous clusters of galaxies, captured by the Chandra X-ray Observatory and Hubble Space Telescope, reveals evidence of dark matter (colorized in blue). Visible matter cannot account for all of the gravitational force holding galaxies together. Galaxies are also held together by an invisible form of matter called dark matter, which can be detected only through its gravitational pull on visible objects. Astronomers determined the location of the dark matter in the image by watching the effect its gravity had on the surrounding visible matter (colorized in pink) and on the light passing through it.

THE INTERSTELLAR MEDIUM

The interstellar medium is all the ordinary matter between star systems in a galaxy. The interstellar medium is made mostly of hydrogen and helium gas, with small amounts of dust made of carbon and other materials. The interstellar medium is pushed away from stars by the stellar wind, which is made up of particles blasted away from the surface of a star. In our solar system, the solar wind of the sun pushes the interstellar medium out to about 9 billion miles (15 billion kilometers) away. As the sun moves through space, the interstellar medium flows around the stellar wind like air flowing around a car on the highway.

Voyager 1 and 2 became the first two spacecraft to pass through the termination shock, a turbulent region where the solar wind begins to mix with the interstellar medium. By 2020, one or both of the probes may cross the heliopause, the boundary where the solar wind becomes too weak to push against the interstellar medium. At this point, the probes will truly leave our solar system.

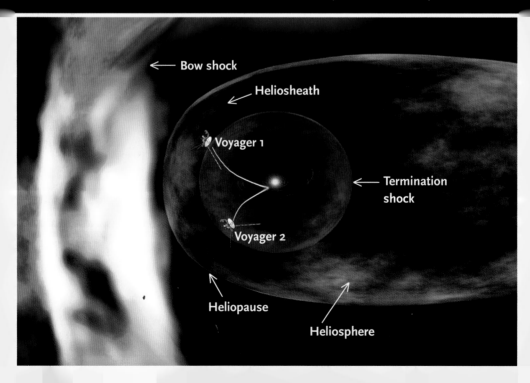

Bow shock
Heliosheath
Voyager 1
Termination shock
Voyager 2
Heliopause
Heliosphere

NOTHING IS EMPTY

Every part of the universe has at least a small amount of matter.

The space between planets in the solar system (1) is relatively dense because of the particles in the solar wind, though the density is much lower than that of the air we breathe. The interstellar medium in the Milky Way (2) is thinner still, but the galaxy's gravity keeps most gas and dust nearby. Matter in the space between galaxies (3) has the lowest density in the universe.

10 million atoms per cubic meter on average
← **1** →

10,000 atoms per cubic meter on average
← **2** →

1 atom per cubic meter on average
← **3** →

THE GALAXY NEXT DOOR

The closest **spiral galaxy** like the Milky Way is the Andromeda Galaxy, about 2.5 million light-years away. Astronomers study Andromeda to get a view of what our galaxy might look like.

THE VEIL OF DUST AND GAS

To study the Milky Way, astronomers must look through our galaxy toward the center or out toward the edge. However, they cannot use **optical** telescopes to see toward the center because thick clouds of dust and gas block the view. Optical telescopes detect only **visible light,** which does not pass through most dust and gas. However, other forms of **electromagnetic radiation** may pass through the dust and gas. Using telescopes that detect **radio waves, infrared light,** and **X rays,** astronomers are able to make observations of the center of the Milky Way.

The Andromeda Galaxy is a large spiral galaxy similar to the Milky Way.

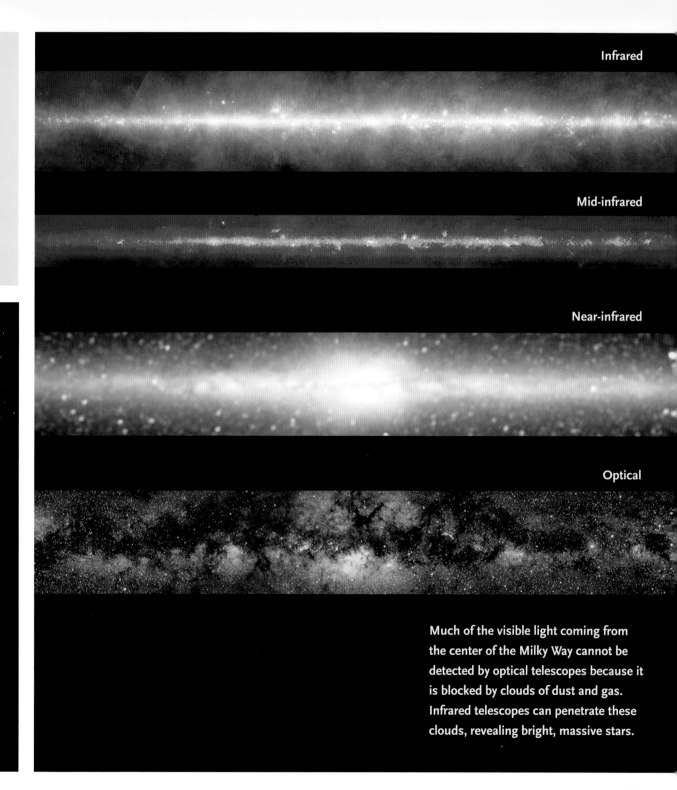

Infrared

Mid-infrared

Near-infrared

Optical

Much of the visible light coming from the center of the Milky Way cannot be detected by optical telescopes because it is blocked by clouds of dust and gas. Infrared telescopes can penetrate these clouds, revealing bright, massive stars.

HOW ARE ASTRONOMERS MAPPING THE MILKY WAY?

OLD MAPS

It is especially hard for astronomers to make accurate maps of the Milky Way. They cannot see what lies in the half of the **galaxy** beyond the central bulge. In the 1950's, astronomers began using special telescopes to detect the **radio waves** that pass through the dust and gas at the center of our galaxy. Astronomers also carefully measured the changes in positions of **stars** as Earth orbited the sun. Calculations based on this information allowed them to make the first maps of the Milky Way. Most maps made before 2008 showed that the Milky Way had four major spiral arms. Astronomers were not sure, however, how many spiral arms the galaxy had.

ONLY TWO ARMS

In 2003, astronomers launched a powerful new telescope called the Spitzer Space Telescope. Spitzer is able to detect **infrared light,** which allows it to detect stars that would otherwise be hidden by dust and gas. Astronomers used observations made by Spitzer to count stars in the spiral arms. They found only two major areas that are tightly packed with stars. These major arms, named Scutum-Centaurus and Perseus, branch into four arms out toward the edge of the galaxy.

The scientists also found that the bar of stars in the center of the galaxy is much longer than they had earlier thought. The two major spiral arms trail out of each end of the bar.

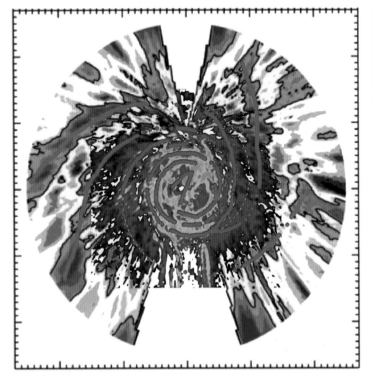

The first detailed map of the *mass* (amount of matter) in the Milky Way shows the denser regions of the spiral arms and central bar in darker red. The map, published in 2009, revealed that two prominent arms extend from the galaxy's core (bluish region) to its outer reaches, where they branch into four arms.

To map the Milky Way and its spiral arms, scientists use such techniques as observation, careful measurements, and mathematics.

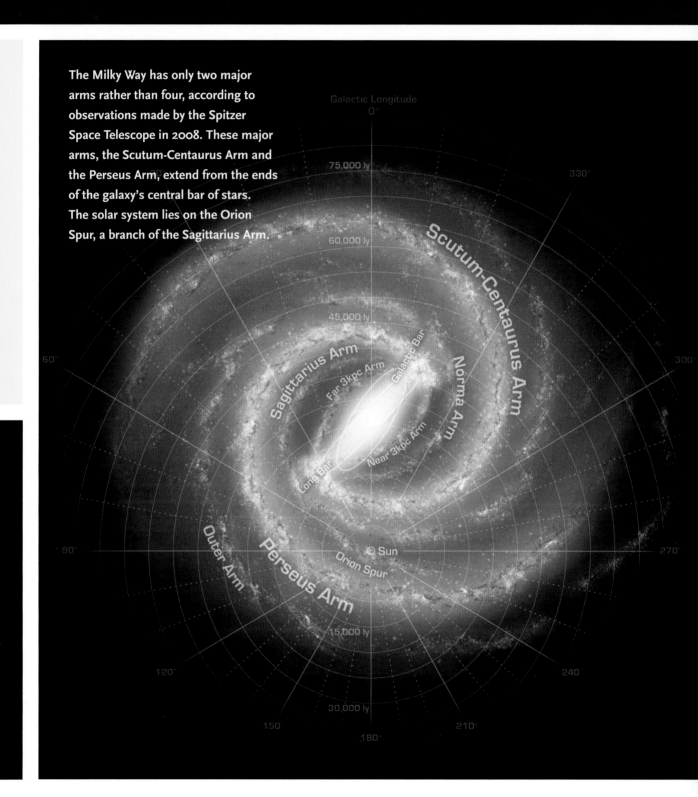

The Milky Way has only two major arms rather than four, according to observations made by the Spitzer Space Telescope in 2008. These major arms, the Scutum-Centaurus Arm and the Perseus Arm, extend from the ends of the galaxy's central bar of stars. The solar system lies on the Orion Spur, a branch of the Sagittarius Arm.

Galactic Longitude
0°

75,000 ly

330°

60,000 ly

Scutum-Centaurus Arm

45,000 ly

Sagittarius Arm

Far 3kpc Arm

Galactic Bar

Norma Arm

60°

300°

Long Bar

Near 3kpc Arm

Sun

Perseus Arm

Outer Arm

Orion Spur

90°

270°

15,000 ly

120°

240°

30,000 ly

150°

210°

180°

ARE NEW STARS FORMING IN THE MILKY WAY?

STELLAR NURSERIES

A **star** begins to form when a cloud of dust and gas collapses from the force of its own **gravity.** Such clouds, called **nebulae,** are made mostly of **hydrogen** and **helium,** in addition to smaller amounts of other **chemical elements.** Large nebulae give birth to many stars. When a nebula produces many new stars, astronomers describe the area as a "stellar nursery."

STAR BIRTH

A star begins to form when part of a nebula gains sufficient **mass** to pull in additional matter through gravity. The more massive the growing ball of dust and gas becomes, the more material it attracts. The ball becomes hotter and denser. Eventually, the ball can only continue to contract gradually, because the matter is packed together so tightly. The ball has become a **protostar.** The temperature and pressure inside the protostar continue to increase until **nuclear fusion** begins. Hydrogen nuclei *fuse* (combine) to make helium. Nuclear fusion gives off enormous amounts of energy, heating the material further. When the protostar is able to sustain nuclear fusion at its center, it becomes a true star.

Massive pillars of dust and gas in the Eagle Nebula act as stellar nurseries, giving birth to stars.

Millions of newborn stars light up a section of the Eagle Nebula, a stellar nursery. After stars form, the energy they give off pushes away the surrounding dust and gas, preventing the formation of other stars nearby.

How a **star** dies depends on its *mass* (amount of matter). Astronomers group stars as high-mass, intermediate-mass, and low-mass stars. The sun is an intermediate-mass star. Throughout most of its life, a star is balanced between **gravity** and pressure. Gravity pulls material in the star inward, driving **nuclear fusion** reactions. Pressure from those reactions balances the pull of gravity, preventing the star's collapse.

The Crab Nebula is the expanding remains of a supernova observed by astronomers in A.D. 1054. The nebula consists of the outer layers of a star that exploded, leaving only a dense, glowing core.

A star remains stable as long as the inward pull of gravity equals the pressure of radiation pushing outward from the interior. This stable phase usually makes up the longest portion of a star's life.

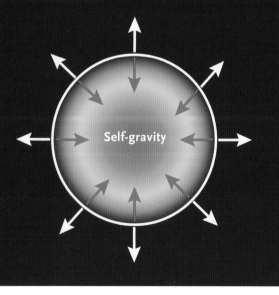

Self-gravity

GOING OUT WITH A BANG

A high-mass star lives a short, spectacular life. It uses up its nuclear fuel quickly, swelling into a **red supergiant.** When the star has exhausted its fuel, nuclear fusion stops, and the star collapses under its own gravity. This collapse sets off a giant explosion called a **supernova.**

After the supernova, an incredibly dense **core** remains. If the core has less than three times the mass of the sun, it becomes a **neutron star.** If the core has more than three times the mass of

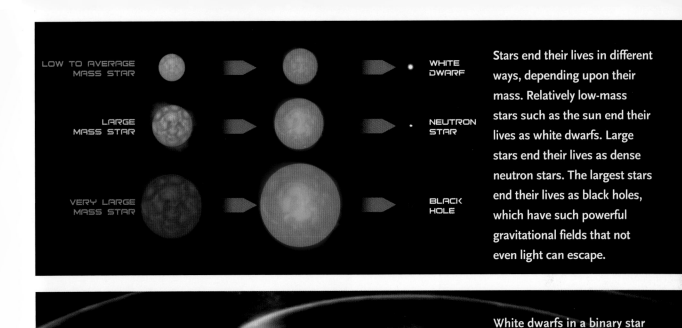

LOW TO AVERAGE MASS STAR			WHITE DWARF
LARGE MASS STAR			NEUTRON STAR
VERY LARGE MASS STAR			BLACK HOLE

Stars end their lives in different ways, depending upon their mass. Relatively low-mass stars such as the sun end their lives as white dwarfs. Large stars end their lives as dense neutron stars. The largest stars end their lives as black holes, which have such powerful gravitational fields that not even light can escape.

White dwarfs in a binary star system orbit each other in an artist's illustration. Eventually, the white dwarfs will cool further and become black dwarfs.

the sun, nothing can stop its collapse. The core becomes a **black hole.**

FADING AWAY

An intermediate-mass star does not die such a violent death. As it uses up its nuclear fuel, it expands into a **red giant.** The star slowly blows its atmosphere out into space. Eventually, only the hot, dense core of the star remains. The star has become a **white dwarf.** The white dwarf glows faintly because of its high temperature. Finally, the white dwarf cools and becomes dark. The star ends its life as a **black dwarf.**

LIVING FOREVER?

A low-mass star lives the longest. In fact, the universe has not existed long enough for a low-mass star to die. Eventually, a low-mass star will follow the same path as an intermediate-mass star. It will become a white dwarf, until finally it fades away as a black dwarf.

THE MEMBERS

There are about 40 known **galaxies** in the Local Group. The galaxies form a *spherical* (round-shaped) **galaxy group** in space. The sphere is about 10 million **light-years** across.

There are three **spiral galaxies** in the Local Group. The Milky Way and the Andromeda Galaxy are the largest. The Triangulum Galaxy is a third, smaller spiral galaxy. The other galaxies are small **dwarf galaxies** with **elliptical** (oval) or **irregular** shapes.

GRAVITY IN THE LOCAL GROUP

Gravity is an important force in the Local Group. Many smaller galaxies orbit the Milky Way or Andromeda like satellites. The gravity of the large galaxies is also pulling **stars** and other matter away from smaller galaxies. Because of gravity, the Milky Way and Andromeda are drawing closer together.

LOCAL SUPERCLUSTER

The Local Group belongs to an even larger collection of groups of galaxies called the Local Supercluster. The **supercluster** is about 100 million light-years across.

The Triangulum Galaxy is a small spiral galaxy in the Local Group.

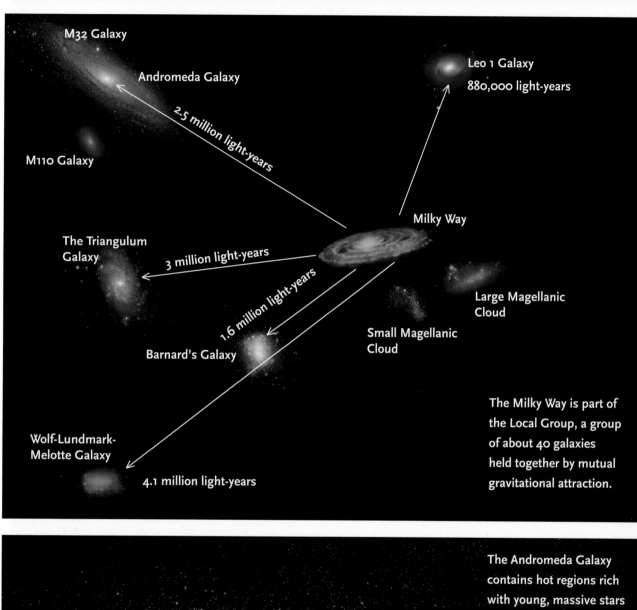

M32 Galaxy

Andromeda Galaxy

M110 Galaxy

Leo 1 Galaxy
880,000 light-years

2.5 million light-years

Milky Way

The Triangulum
Galaxy

3 million light-years

1.6 million light-years

Large Magellanic
Cloud

Small Magellanic
Cloud

Barnard's Galaxy

The Milky Way is part of
the Local Group, a group
of about 40 galaxies
held together by mutual
gravitational attraction.

Wolf-Lundmark-
Melotte Galaxy

4.1 million light-years

The Andromeda Galaxy
contains hot regions rich
with young, massive stars
(red) and cooler regions
with developing stars
shrouded in dust (blue),
as shown in a composite
image made with ultraviolet
and infrared data.

The Milky Way 49

WHAT IS A GLOBULAR CLUSTER?

MANY GLOBULAR CLUSTERS

There are many **globular clusters** in the Milky Way. Most of them are outside the disk of the galaxy. **Gravity** holds globular clusters tightly together in the shape of a sphere a few tens of **light-years** in diameter. By the early 2000's, astronomers had discovered more than 155 globular clusters in the Milky Way.

OLD STARS

Astronomers believe that globular clusters formed early in the history of the universe. **Stars** in globular clusters are mainly made of **hydrogen** and **helium.** Stars that formed later contain such **elements** as carbon and oxygen. Globular clusters in the Milky Way indicate that our galaxy is nearly as old as the universe.

A globular cluster (arrow) shines brightly in an infrared image taken by the Spitzer Space Telescope. Clouds of dust and gas block the light from the cluster in a photograph (right, inset) taken by a telescope that collects visible light.

Area in visible light

A globular cluster is a large, tightly packed group of stars held together by gravity. A globular cluster can have from 10,000 to several million stars.

The globular cluster NGC 6397 is one of the closest of these objects to Earth, at 7,200 light-years away. The cluster is also one of the densest, with about 400,000 stars.

The globular cluster M12 loses stars as it passes through the disk of the Milky Way, as shown in an artist's illustration. The stars become part of the halo of stars that surrounds the galaxy.

WHAT IS AN OPEN CLUSTER?

YOUNGER STARS

Most **open clusters** have an irregular shape and are about 5 to 20 **light-years** across. Open clusters are mainly in the disk of the Milky Way. They are held together by **gravity.** More than 2 percent of the material in **stars** consists of **chemical elements** heavier than **hydrogen** and **helium.** These heavier elements tell astronomers that open clusters contain younger stars. Heavy elements formed when early stars in the Milky Way exploded. Only **supernovae** reach the energies needed for **nuclear fusion** reactions to produce heavy elements. The explosions spread the elements throughout clouds of dust and gas. When these clouds collapsed into the stars of the open cluster, the heavier elements became part of the new stars.

MOVING GROUPS

Another type of star grouping, called a **moving group,** contains stars that are not held together by **gravity.** However, the stars in a moving group have several things in common. They move in a similar direction and at a similar speed, are made of the same elements, and are about the same age. Generally, moving groups were once open clusters, until the stars in them drifted apart. Perhaps the best-known moving group is in Ursa Major.

Ursa Major

Most of the stars that form the constellation Ursa Major, also known as the Big Dipper, are members of a moving group that is about 80 light-years away.

An open cluster is a grouping of a few hundred stars loosely bound by gravity.

The stars of the Pleiades form an open cluster that is slowly drifting apart into a moving group. Interstellar gas around the stars appears in green and red in a false-color infrared image taken by the Spitzer Space Telescope.

THE BIG BANG

Most astronomers believe that the universe began in an explosion called the **big bang.** The matter in the universe was distributed evenly, except for tiny variations that gave the universe a kind of lumpiness. Scientists can still detect these variations in the **cosmic microwave background (CMB) radiation.** The CMB radiation is the oldest **electromagnetic radiation** that scientists can detect. Today, the distribution of **galaxies** matches variations in the CMB radiation, meaning that the earliest clumps of matter gave rise to galaxies.

COLLIDING GALAXIES

The Milky Way and other galaxies likely formed through a series of collisions. Clouds of gas first formed around dense areas of a mysterious, invisible substance called **dark matter.** Astronomers call these bodies protogalaxies.

Protogalaxies pulled in surrounding matter through **gravity,** but they also attracted each other. When two protogalaxies collided, bursts of **star** formation began. Repeated collisions between small galaxies eventually formed large galaxies such as the Milky Way.

Variations in the cosmic background microwave radiation, detected by the Cosmic Background Explorer (COBE) spacecraft, match the positions of galaxies in the universe today.

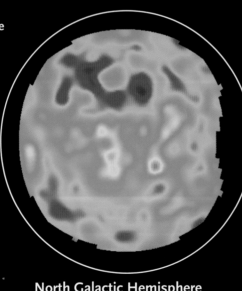

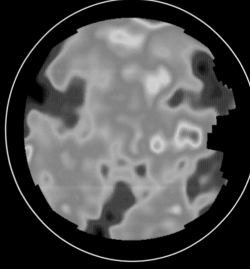

North Galactic Hemisphere   **South Galactic Hemisphere**

Astronomers believe that the universe began in an explosion called the big bang. The Milky Way formed soon after from a cloud of gas and dark matter that pulled in surrounding material through gravity.

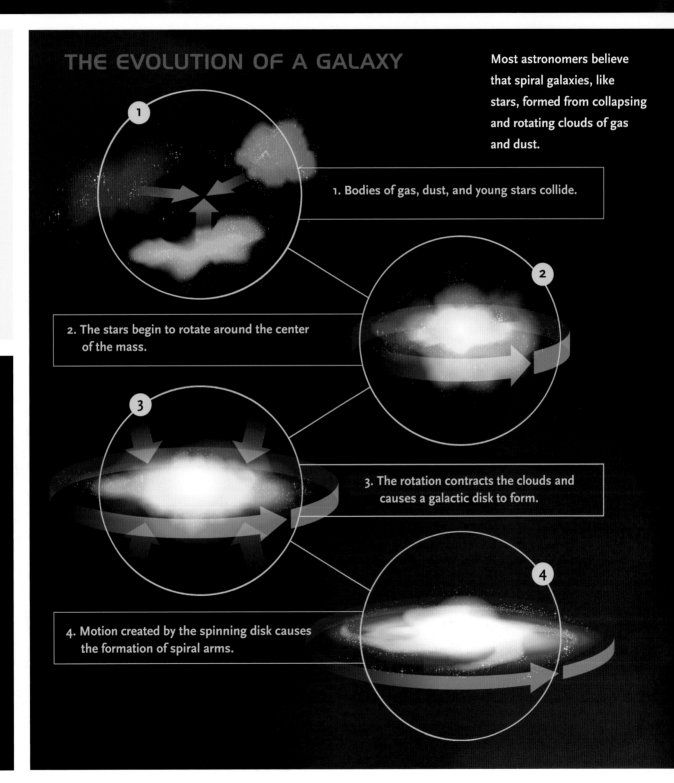

THE EVOLUTION OF A GALAXY

Most astronomers believe that spiral galaxies, like stars, formed from collapsing and rotating clouds of gas and dust.

1. Bodies of gas, dust, and young stars collide.

2. The stars begin to rotate around the center of the mass.

3. The rotation contracts the clouds and causes a galactic disk to form.

4. Motion created by the spinning disk causes the formation of spiral arms.

GALACTIC CANNIBAL

Powerful telescopes found evidence in the early 2000's that the Milky Way has consumed several smaller **galaxies.** Even now, the Milky Way is consuming two nearby **dwarf galaxies.** The **gravity** of our galaxy is also pulling matter from the Large and Small Magellanic Clouds, two small galaxies. In a few billion years, the Milky Way will likely collide with Andromeda, another large **spiral galaxy.**

EVOLVING BAR

The bar at the center of the galaxy has also evolved. When the Milky Way was young, it may not have had the bar of **stars** that exists in the core today. Instead, all the stars in the center of the galaxy had a circular orbit. Over time, their orbits become flatter and more oval-shaped, forming a bar. More than 50 percent of spiral galaxies have central bars.

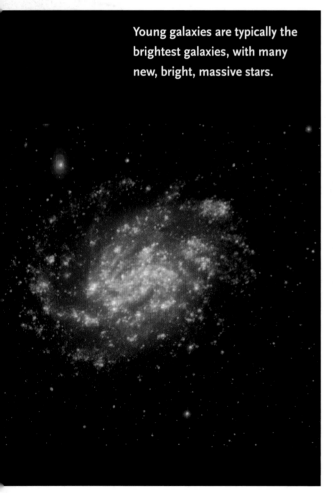

Young galaxies are typically the brightest galaxies, with many new, bright, massive stars.

As galaxies age, star formation slows, and many stars become dim white dwarfs or neutron stars.

At least three giant streams of stars wrap around the Milky Way, shown in an artist's illustration based on infrared data collected by the Spitzer Space Telescope. The streams, which are from 13,000 to 130,000 light-years from Earth, are likely the remains of ancient star clusters ripped apart by the gravitational force of the Milky Way.

In old age, galaxies become dim because most of their stars have burned out.

The sun

HOW THE MILKY WAY MAY END

The Milky Way and its huge spiral neighbor, the Andromeda Galaxy, are speeding toward each other at about 75 miles (120 kilometers) per second. When the two galaxies collide, the Milky Way will be changed forever.

The force of the collision will fling some stars out of their orbits. Giant clouds of gas and dust will crash into each other, creating shock waves that trigger the birth of new stars. The collision may last about 5.5 billion years. But the sun and Earth may not be greatly affected because the distance between stars in galaxies is so great.

The collision will not begin for about 2 billion years. When it is over, the Milky Way and Andromeda will no longer be spiral galaxies. They will become one new elliptical galaxy.

The Antennae Galaxies are two spiral galaxies that are merging. The galaxies are bright because the collision has caused an explosion of star formation. In time, the galaxies will likely become one large elliptical galaxy.

The Milky Way is a large galaxy with a powerful gravitational field. Our galaxy strips stars and other matter from nearby dwarf galaxies. It also consumes dense clouds of gas (shaded red) from deep space.

Galaxies collide and merge over many millions of years, greatly changing in shape and brightness. However, stars within the galaxies rarely collide because ▼ the distance between them is so vast.

GLOSSARY

Big bang – The cosmic explosion that began the expansion of the universe.

Binary stars – Stars that orbit around each other.

Black dwarf – The dark remnant of a white dwarf that is too cold to give off light.

Black hole – The collapsed core of a massive star. The gravity of a black hole is so strong that not even light can escape.

Chemical element – Any substance that contains only one kind of atom. Hydrogen and helium are both chemical elements.

Core – The dense, hot center of a star.

Cosmic microwave background (CMB) radiation – The most ancient electromagnetic radiation in the universe. Variations in the CMB correspond to the distribution of galaxies in the universe today.

Dark matter – A mysterious form of matter that does not reflect or absorb light. The majority of matter in the universe is dark matter.

Dwarf galaxy – A small galaxy, containing only several billion stars.

Electromagnetic radiation – Any form of light, ranging from radio waves, to microwaves, to infrared light, to visible light, to ultraviolet light, to X rays, to gamma rays.

Elliptical galaxy – A galaxy with a shape that somewhat resembles a flattened globe.

Exoplanet – Any planet in orbit around a star other than the sun.

Galaxy – A vast system of stars, gas, dust, and other matter held together in space by mutual gravitational attraction.

Galaxy group – A concentration of dozens of galaxies held together by gravity.

Globular cluster – A large group of stars held together by gravity. A globular cluster may contain tens of thousands to several million stars packed together in a sphere only tens of light-years in diameter.

Gravity – The force of attraction that acts between all objects because of their mass.

Helium – The second simplest chemical element. Helium is produced through the nuclear fusion of hydrogen.

Hydrogen – The simplest chemical element. Hydrogen is the most abundant substance in the universe. It fuels most stars.

Infrared light – A form of light with long wavelengths. Also called heat radiation. Infrared is invisible to the unaided eye.

Irregular galaxy – A galaxy with a patchy, disorderly appearance.

Light pollution – Artificial light that blots out the faint light of stars.

Light-year – The distance light travels in a vacuum in one year. One light-year is equal to 5.88 trillion miles (9.46 trillion kilometers).

Mass – The amount of matter in an object.

Moving group – A group of stars of similar age and with similar direction and speed. These stars are no longer held together by gravity.

Nebula – A cloud of dust and gas in space.

Neutron star – A star that has collapsed into a small area with extremely high mass. Neutron stars form from the remains of massive stars that have exploded in supernovae.

Nuclear fusion – The combination of two or more atomic *nuclei* (cores) to form the nucleus of a heavier element. Nuclear fusion releases the energy that powers stars.

Open cluster – A group of stars held together by gravity. Open clusters typically contain younger and fewer stars than do globular clusters.

Optical – Of or relating to visible light.

Planet – A large, round heavenly body that orbits a star.

Planetary system – A group of heavenly bodies consisting of a star and the planets and other objects orbiting around it.

Protostar – A ball-shaped object that has collected from the dust and gas of a nebula but has not yet become a true star.

Pulsar – A neutron star that gives off regular pulses of electromagnetic radiation.

Radio waves – The form of light with the longest wavelengths. Radio waves are invisible to the unaided eye.

Red dwarf – A small, relatively cool star that glows with a dim, reddish light. Red dwarfs range in mass from about 1/12 to 1/2 the mass of the sun.

Red giant – A large, bright star that glows with a reddish light. When its fuel is exhausted, a red giant becomes a white dwarf.

Red supergiant – A huge, extremely bright star that glows with a reddish light. When its fuel is exhausted, a red supergiant explodes in a supernova.

Solar system – The planetary system that includes the sun and Earth.

Spectrum, spectra – Light divided into its different wavelengths. A spectrum may provide astronomers with information about a heavenly body's chemical composition, motion, and distance.

Spiral galaxy – A galaxy with a thin, disk-like structure and sweeping arms of stars wrapped about the galaxy's center.

Star – A huge, shining ball in space that produces a tremendous amount of light and other forms of energy.

Supercluster – A giant collection of galaxy groups and clusters containing tens of thousands of galaxies.

Supernova, supernovae – An exploding star that can become billions of times as bright as the sun before gradually fading from view. A supernova occurs when a massive star uses up all its fuel.

Visible light – The form of light human beings can see with their eyes.

White dwarf – A star that has exhausted its fuel. A typical white dwarf has about 60 percent as much mass as the sun but is no larger than Earth.

X rays – A form of light with short wavelengths. X rays are invisible to the unaided eye.

FOR MORE INFORMATION

WEB SITES

MultiWavelength Milky Way

http://mwmw.gsfc.nasa.gov

Enter the "Education" portal to access images and descriptions of the Milky Way, from NASA's Goddard Space Flight Center.

StarChild: A Learning Center for Young Astronauts

http://starchild.gsfc.nasa.gov

A Web site from NASA that provides basic information about our solar system and the universe beyond, with suggestions for classroom activities.

Windows to the Universe

http://www.windows.ucar.edu/windows.html

Emphasizes our solar system, its planets, asteroids and comets, and meteor activity. Enter "milky way" in the search box for a list of relevant articles.

BOOKS

11 Planets: A New View of the Solar System by David A. Aguilar (National Geographic Society, 2008)

The Milky Way by Steve Kortenkamp (Capstone Press, 2008)

The Milky Way and Other Galaxies by Dana Meachen Rau (Compass Point Books, 2005)

Mysteries of the Milky Way from *Scientific American* (Rosen Publishing, 2008)

Planets, Stars, and Galaxies: A Visual Encyclopedia of Our Universe by David A. Aguilar (National Geographic Society, 2007)

INDEX

ACKNOWLEDGMENTS

The publishers acknowledge the following sources for illustrations. Credits read from top to bottom, left to right, on their respective pages. All illustrations, maps, charts, and diagrams were prepared by the staff unless otherwise noted.

Cover: © Wally Pacholka, AstroPics

1 © Jon Lomberg, Photo Researchers

4-5 NOAO

6-7 Bruno Gilli, ESO; © Jon Lomberg, Photo Researchers

8-9 © Asian Art & Archaeology/Corbis; Mary Evans Picture Library; Astronomer observing the Milky Way, cover of a book of astronomy, *Heaven and Earth,* by W. Meyer (1908) color litho (Archives Charmet/Bridgeman Art Library)

10-11 NASA

12-13 P. Cinzano, F. Falchi (Univ. of Padova), C. D. Elvidge (NOAA National Geophysical Data Center, Boulder). © Royal Astronomical Society. Reproduced from the *Monthly Notices of the RAS* by permission of Blackwell Science; The Huntington Library, San Marino, CA; Dave Jurasevich, Mt. Wilson Observatory

14-15 ESO, S. Gillessen; ESO, S. Brunier; WORLD BOOK illustration by Matt Carrington

16-17 James S. Bullock & Kathryn V. Johnston (2005); © Shigemi Numazawa, Atlas Photo Bank/Photo Researchers; © HowStuffWorks

18-19 WORLD BOOK illustration by Rob Wood; The Isaac Newton Group of Telescopes, La Palma, and Simon Dye; Cardiff Univ.; WORLD BOOK illustration by Matt Carrington/NASA

20-21 WORLD BOOK illustration by Rob Wood; NASA/CXC/M. Weiss; ESA/MSU/M. Sun, XMM

22-23 NASA/JPL-Caltech/S. Stolovy (SSC/Caltech); NASA/CXC/MIT/F. K. Baganoff

24-25 ESO; NASA/WMAP Science Team

26-27 NASA/JPL-Caltech/R. Hurt (SSC); NASA/CXC/M. Weiss; WORLD BOOK illustration by Rob Wood

28-29 © Helmut K. Wimmer, National Geographic Society

30-31 W. M. Keck Observatory; NASA and G. Bacon (STScI)

32-33 Digitized Sky Survey, U. K. Schmidt Image/STScI; WORLD BOOK illustration by Don Di Sante; © A. Fujii

34-35 © Popperfoto/Getty Images; © Margaret Bourke-White, Time & Life Pictures/Getty Images

36-37 WORLD BOOK illustration by Luke Haddock; NASA/CXC/CfA/STScI/Magellan/Univ. of Ariz./ESO

38-39 NASA; NASA; NASA, ESA, H. Hammel (SSI, Boulder, CO) and the Jupiter Impact Team; NASA/ESA/L. Bradley (JHU)/R. Bouwens (UCSC)/H. Ford (JHU)/G. Illingworth (UCSC); NASA/JPL-Caltech/R. Gutermuth (Harvard-Smithsonian Center for Astrophysics); X-ray: NASA/CXC/Univ. of Maryland/A. S. Wilson et al.; Optical: Pal. Obs. DSS; IR: NASA/JPL-Caltech; VLA: NRAO/AUI/NSF; X-ray: NASA/CXC/Wesleyan Univ./R. Kilgard et al.; UV: NASA/JPL-Caltech; Optical: NASA/ESA/S. Beckwith & Hubble Heritage Team (STScI/AURA); IR: NASA/JPL-Caltech/ Univ. of AZ/R. Kennicutt

40-41 NASA/JPL/California Institute of Technology; NASA

42-43 © Martin Pohl, Iowa State Univ. NASA/JPL-Caltech/R. Hurt (SSC-Caltech)

44-45 NASA/STSi; A. Rector and B. A. Wolpa, NRAO/AUI/AURA/NSF

46-47 WORLD BOOK illustration by Don Di Sante; NASA/CXC/J. Hester, ASU (X-ray), NASA/ESA/J. Hester & A. Loll, ASU (optical), NASA/JPL-Caltech/R. Gehrz, Univ. Minn. (infrared); WORLD BOOK illustration; GSFC/D. Berry

48-49 NASA/JPL-Caltech; WORLD BOOK illustration by Don Di Sante/NASA; NASA/JPL-Caltech

50-51 NASA/JPL-Caltech/H. Kobulnicky (Univ. of Wyoming); NASA and F. Paresce/ESA and Guido de Marchi; ESO

52-53 © Akira Fujii and David Malin; NASA/JPL-Caltech/ J. Stauffer (SSC/Caltech)

54-55 NASA; © HowStuffWorks

56-57 NASA/JPL-Caltech/Las Campanas; NASA/JPL-Caltech/CTIO; NASA/JPL-Caltech/CTIO; NASA/JPL-Caltech/R. Hurt (SSC)

58-59 NASA, ESA, and B. Whitmore (STSI) and James Long (ESA/Hubble); Bill Saxton, NRAO/AUI/NSF; NASA, ESA, and The Hubble Heritage Team (STSci)